Seeing the Blue Between

Advice and Inspiration for Young Poets

Seeing the Blue Between

Advice and Inspiration for Young Poets

compiled by
Paul B. Janeczko

CANDLEWICK PRESS
CAMBRIDGE, MASSACHUSETTS

First edition 2002

Library of Congress Cataloging-in-Publication Data

Seeing the blue between : advice and inspiration for young poets /
compiled by Paul B. Janeczko. — 1st ed.
p.   cm.
ISBN 0-7636-0881-5
1. Children's poetry, American. 2. Poetry—Authorship—Juvenile literature.
[1. American poetry—Collections. 2. Poetry—Authorship.
3. Creative writing.] I. Janeczko, Paul B.
PS586.3. S44 2002
811'.60809282—dc21   2001025882

2 4 6 8 10 9 7 5 3 1

Printed in the United States of America

This book was typeset in Giovanni and Stone Sans.

Candlewick Press
2067 Massachusetts Avenue
Cambridge, Massachusetts 02140

visit us at www.candlewick.com

For my mother,
whose creativity in the kitchen
nurtured me, body and soul.
Sto lat!

P. B. J.

Contents

Seeing the Blue Between

Dear Poet,

How can I become a better writer?

  Young poets who read my books often write to me with that question. I usually tell them to do two things: write a lot of poetry and read a lot of poetry. The letters and poems I've assembled in *Seeing the Blue Between* should add one more thing to every young writer's "to do" list: listen to the advice of poets who have spent years practicing their craft.

  I hope the poets in this book inspire you. And I hope you learn from their words. I know that I have. I've learned that there is always something new to try with my writing. I think that's part of the kick of writing — trying something new and seeing what happens when we do. Some of the poets here offer practical writing suggestions. Others offer ways to look at the world in a new way. But all of them want you to have the confidence to take risks when you write.

  So curl up in your favorite reading spot — be it that soft chair in your room or the corner table in the school cafeteria — take a deep breath, and leap into the blue between.

Seeing Your Poetry

When you're a young poet it's hard at times to figure out what it is that you should write about. You may feel as if you haven't lived long enough or learned enough — or at least that is what some people may tell you. Don't listen to them. In fact, whenever someone tells you that you can't do something as a writer, take that as a challenge, not a roadblock. Some of the best things I've ever done came about because someone told me I couldn't do them. Instead of turning away, I opened my eyes wider to see a way through.

I started writing poems when I was in second grade, but I didn't get really serious about it until college. By then, I was known as an athlete, a "dumb jock" to some. My creative writing instructor took one look at me, a 200-pound heavyweight wrestler, and concluded I was in the wrong class. "Give it up," he said. "You'll never be a poet."

So did I give it up? No way, Jose! From then on I did nothing but write poetry, sometimes twenty poems a day. And what did I write about? I wrote what I saw. I kept a journal with me constantly. If I was riding with a friend I'd write about the things I saw as we rolled through the hills around the Cornell University campus or looked out at the long, blue arm of Cayuga Lake. I wrote about the hawks hovering over the cornfields, the mounds that were the remains of old Iroquois villages, the rusting cars in junkyards, even the way a dump ripples with life after dark when the rats start to move.

One secret to remember is that every writer — whether they're a famous poet or a beginner — starts with a blank page (or computer screen). But where others see nothing, poets envision something. One word at a time, a vision takes shape. And the more you write, the more you see. I went into Cornell's campus gallery to look at paintings and wrote poems describing what I saw and what I thought the artist must have seen. I listened to music, then found words to describe the pictures those sounds drew in my mind. I closed my eyes, seeing once again in my memory what it was like in my grandmother's kitchen on the cold winter morning when the old cat had just given birth to a litter of kittens behind the old cast iron wood stove. Everything I saw became poetry.

By the end of the month, buried in my poems, my writing instructor threw up his hands. "Bruchac," he said. "I was wrong. You *can* write poetry."

I'd seen my way to victory. If you keep your eyes open—those in your head and those in your heart—you may do the same.

Song to the Firefly

Beside the great beautiful lake
named Gitchee-gummi,
the sound of voices
drifts up into the summer sky,
as the children of the Anishinabe
chase the fireflies,
singing this song.

Small white-fire being,
small white-fire being,
give me light
around my lodge
before I sleep,
before I sleep,
before I sleep—ewee!

Small white-fire being,
small white-fire being,
light my way with your fire,
light my way with your fire,
before I sleep,
before I sleep.

Small white-fire being,
small white-fire being,
let your light
carry me
into sleep.

Longhouse Song

Elm bark is my skin
bent saplings my bones
my mouth that draws
in the living wind
is the door to the coming of sun.

My breath
is the smoke
rising up to join sky.
My heart is the fire
in the circle of stones.

My eyes, my spirit
and my thoughts
belong to those
who keep close to the earth
their dreams held
by the circle of seasons.

SIV CEDERING

There is a place where all my poems

begin. It is not a nook where I hide with a book. It is not a chair or a bench where I sit. It is a place hidden inside where dreams can hide and thoughts fly freer than kites in the sky.

In this place I can find a poem, a song, or a film can spin out a story that has never been seen. The music I hear in my mind is more complex than anything I can play or whistle or sing, yet I find I can follow its sound. Is a lyric attaching itself? Shall I repeat that chorus or verse? How will that theme unfold? What else will that melody do?

Sometimes I stay there for a minute, sometimes for an hour or two. I visualize a sculpture, design a house, jot down a word or a line or a rhyme. For when I have sat like that and peeked in my unwritten book, I often wonder if I can catch the poem that's beginning, the notes I hear, the story that has caught my attention and is pulling me along. Then I take hold of a pencil and write down a phrase or more. I hit a chord on the piano, pick out a note or four. I sketch a group of sculptures, add water, and watch a fountain grow. I scribble notes in the margin, to remind myself later of what I should do.

The best part of all this dreaming is letting it flow — I know that if I run with the kite and let out the string, the treasure that has hidden in my mind will fly, will go higher and higher. Look at it riding the wind. Look at it go!

Don't for a moment think that people who write and compose, make movies, poems, or songs are very different from you. The difference, if it exists, might just be that they take time to imagine what they would like to do.

So if you want to write a poem, paint a picture, plan a house and make blueprints, compose a pop song or a symphony, develop a narrative for a movie or a play, consider beginning by just sitting and thinking — and follow that thought, on and on, further and yet further to a place where no one has ever been before.

The Changeling

One day you see it so clearly.
You could not really be their child.
Your parents would know it,
if they could look inside you.
Despite what relatives say
about mother's nose or smile
or father's eyes and toes,
the mirror tells the truth;
you are different.

At first you try to hide the fact.
You are glad you have been taken in
and have a place to sleep,
and eat. But soon,
you no longer want their charity.
You see through their affection.
You hear the phony note
in the assurance that of course
you are theirs, of course
they love you. You know better.

You look for a likeness in the faces
of strangers. You search for kinship
in books. You look at maps
that can show you the way.
You definitely know you are not
meant to do what your mother does,
your father. Even your supposed siblings,

however friendly and familiar,
cannot understand what occupies
your heart. So you choose to sleep
under the bed or in the attic.
You wish you had been left
to be brought up by the wolves,
or that the floating city
will soon return to collect
its lost children. You want
your real parents to finally come,
clutching the worn and torn documents
from the orphanage, to embrace you
with tear-stained faces.

Meanwhile you wait,
preparing. You study
your chosen subject. You write
your poems. You feed
the original flame that burns
inside you, because you know
that is the only way
you will get to live the life
that is meant to be yours.

KALLI DAKOS

I was sitting at lunch

with a group of students when Tony looked down at his sandwich and yelled, "Someone took a bite out of my peanut butter and potato chips sandwich and it wasn't me!"

I was a tired teacher that day and didn't want to deal with problems, but the poet inside of me began to bubble up in excitement. There was a story here, a mystery, and I had to check it out. We never did figure out where that bite went, but together we wrote the poem "Who Took a Bite Out of Tony's Sandwich?" And later that week I tried my first peanut butter and potato chips sandwich.

It's the poet inside of me who knows how to live. It's the poet inside of me who is wide awake, and ready to embrace the beauty, the challenges, and the mysteries in life. It's the poet inside of me who celebrates living on a daily basis, and finds extraordinary joys in very ordinary moments.

Take pencils, for example. Who would think there might be a gold mine of writing possibilities in plain old pencils? But pencils, like the one I found in my driveway, have stories too, and some of them are tragic:

Under a car   squished out flat   awful to end   life like that.

Or the poor pencil that ended up in the toilet.

My pencil is a mess,
Because I heard it drop,
Into the toilet
With a plip, plip, plop!

If I weren't a poet, I would have missed the little girl who had glued a rainbow of colored yarn to the top of her pencil so it would be as pretty as the fancy ones her friends had purchased in the stores, and I would have definitely missed the problem that the bright yellow five-foot styrofoam pencil had:

I may be pretty; I may be smart.
But I am a pencil without a part.

I may be lovely; I may be bright,
But I'm a pencil that just can't write.

If there is a gold mine of poetry in pencils, then there must be buried treasures all around us: in the book bags we lug to school, the snowflakes that fall, the trees outside classroom windows, the games we play in gym, the stories we tell at lunch, and the secrets we hide in our hearts.

As I write this letter, I am looking outside my study window at the bank of my river. A man is throwing a ball to a dog, and by accident, he throws it in the water. The dog runs to the water's edge, stops, and looks at the ball floating away. I watch in awe. Will the dog jump in the water or not? A strange thought crosses my mind — at least he doesn't have to worry about a bathing suit.

The water is cold, but the dog makes the courageous choice and jumps in. He paddles to the ball and brings it back to the owner, ready to play the game again.

I begin to write my next poem:

"Dogs Don't Have to Wear Bathing Suits"

Kalli Dakos

My Writing Is an Awful Mess

My writing is an awful mess,
And my teacher asked me why.
"I zoom through my assignments,"
I told her with a sigh.

"I want to finish all this work
So I can yack with friends,
I simply cannot wait until
The school day finally ends.

"I never check my spelling and
Punctuation, I don't try,
For if I spent my time on these,
My . . . social life would die.

"It's talking with my friends each day
That keeps my whole world bright,
And I don't want to give this up,
Just to get my schoolwork right."

I'd Mark with the Sunshine

If I were a teacher,
I wouldn't mark in red,
Because red reminds me
Of blood that
Oozes out of cuts,
And fire engines that
Rush to fight blazes
So hot you could
Die in them,
And STOP signs that
Warn you of danger.

If I were a teacher
I'd mark in yellow—
For corn muffins,
Mustard on a fat hot dog,
Gardens of dandelions,
And sunbeams that
Dance on daffodils.

If I were a teacher,
I'd throw out
My STOP pen,
And I'd mark with
The sunshine itself!
To give light to an *A,*
Warmth to a *C,*
And hope to an *F.*

MICHAEL DUGAN

Letter to a Young Poet

Love words,
play with them,
find the meanings of those you don't know.
Learn to recognize
descriptive words,
active words,
evocative words,
reflective words—
all manner of words
for all manner of purposes.
Decide whether you like to write in rhyme
or in other forms.
Experiment,
invent words,
invent forms,
harness ideas,
fish for images
and metaphors.
Express your ideas
in words and forms
that suit you.

Find your own voice
even if it takes hard work
and many hours.
Traveling to a poem
is a journey to be enjoyed.

P.S. I meant to start with this but decided to finish with it:
Read other poets' poems, learn from them, and delight in
them.

Michael Dugan

Don't Tell Me

Don't tell me about your problems
for I've a few of my own,
my nose has grown a pimple,
my toenails are ingrown.

My knees are very knobbly,
my legs are skin and bone,
my bathers have a hole
where things should not be shown.

My teeth are quite misshapen,
my hair is falling out,
my doctor now suspects that
my left foot suffers gout.

My stomach's fat and hairy,
my chest is thin and weak,
a boil is now appearing
upon my right-hand cheek.

So, forget about your problems
on this sunny seaside day,
and also, please, I beg you,
put that camera away.

Bleak Prospect

When I went swimming in the sea
I didn't spot the whale,
so I was unsuspecting
when it flipped me with its tail.

It sent me flying right into
the jaws of a large shark.
My left leg's gone, my right is going,
my future's looking dark.

ROBERT FARNSWORTH

Dear Poet,

So you want to write poems. So did I, from when I was
about thirteen. And I've been doing so ever since. Here's
some of what I've learned in thirty years of writing.

Look. Listen. Smell. Touch. Remember. Suppose. Be
alert, as if you had just arrived in your life. Keep the corner
of your eye on things, so they stay as strange to you as they
really are. Picture these things, so you can sneak up on them
and see them, say them, seize them. Poetry names the secrets
you didn't know you were keeping. So surprise yourself.
Follow one wild line with another—the mood, the logic, the
sound or picture of that line—follow where it leads. You'll
see what the poem is shaping up to say or mean, and you
will want to shape it some more later. But for now, be
alert—you've just arrived in this poem you're making, and
the whole world spins around its making, while it lasts.

And what do you make poems with? You make poems
with words and sentences and lines. Words first. Collect
them, whisper them, shout them, savor them in your mouth.
Open them. These words will arrive in you like seeds, with
memories and plans for many lives inside of them. Listen
to them. Be alive in your language—be graceful, sincere,

sarcastic, smooth, rough. And explore other languages, as much as you can of those spoken in other places, and as many as you can of the little ones (mechanics, seamanship, botany, cooking, etc) inside of your own.

READ. READ. READ. Poetry, of course, but also fiction, history, and science. Find a quiet place to read aloud, to listen to the shapes of words and of sentences on the air. That way, when you make your own poems, the music you have been singing will show you how to sing. Make sentences of different lengths and tunes, and make them strong—use active verbs and the exact names of things. Say your sentences out loud to yourself, and break them into lines that reveal some different tones of voice—wonder or anger or laughter or sadness—a mixture of feelings that your poem, and only your poem, can name.

Why make poems? Because you love reading and making them. Because for you the world stands up and lives most vividly in poems. Your poems probably won't pay your bills, but one at a time, they'll give shape and bring surprise to your life and to your readers' lives. And that's plenty. Make strange. Be true. Good Luck.

Robert Farnsworth

Yard Sale

Gold-plate goblets freckled
with tarnish, disconsolate
pajamas, infant shoes, curling
irons, somebody's ancient

block flute, a candlestick grove,
bakelite coasters, egg poachers,
7 rubber sandals. Scruffy dolls
and accessories, board games

from whose battered boxes
children still look up with glee.
Two bald lamps, a basketball
and dumbbells, a toaster's chrome

full of early leaves, and tilted
like a grimy satellite inside
a crate, a two-stroke engine.
Now at last admitted to my

neighbor's back lawn, which
I've longed to cut across for years,
I see a tuft of grass and violets,
violets, growing, up in that

elm's clavicle, a little island
world in the air, where the trunk
divides. I wouldn't know how
to tell her of the delight I find

in this. But I think I'll buy that
small stack of teaspoons, just
so I can linger, picking up this
language, whose every word has

finally toppled over in one case
or tense or mood. Everything as is.

RALPH FLETCHER

Digging for Mystery

When I write poems I try to get at the mystery of my subject. When I use that word — *mystery* — I mean the truth about the subject that isn't obvious, that's under the surface. I try to dig down to that rich layer of mystery. Sometimes when I get an idea, I dig down and find — nothing. Oh, well. Maybe the mystery wasn't there, or maybe I wasn't ready to find it. Either way, I move on and write about something else.

Poets find mystery in everyday things and objects: a baby's head, your grandmother's loose-skinned hand, a key chain full of keys sprawled on the counter.

For instance, I am right-handed. When I look at my left hand I see the obvious: my left hand. But it strikes me that compared to my right hand, my left is pathetic. It can't do anything! I can barely throw, draw, write, or eat with it. That might provide the idea for a poem.

Not everything feels mysterious, of course, but when I find something that does, I jot it down in my writer's notebook before I forget. I'm working on a poetry book that will be titled *Have You Been to the Beach Lately?* It's about a family that goes to the beach around midafternoon, when everyone is leaving, and stays until after sunset. I chose that time frame because that's when the beach reveals its mysterious side: the long slanting shadows, the fiery corridor of light leading to the setting sun.

I went to the beach and sat for a long time with my writer's notebook in hand. I jotted down ideas for poems. As the beach emptied out, I began to see more old people walking along the shore. At one point I saw an old man with a metal detector, looking for coins. I have always been fascinated by those metal detectors (isn't everybody?) and I wrote down this idea in my notebook. I watched this man for a long time. Human beings are searchers, and this man was looking for something. As I watched, I let my imagination go and wondered what he might be looking for. Here's the poem that resulted:

Man with a Metal Detector

> He looks like the kind of guy
> people make fun of:
> the bulky earphones,
> that weird contraption,
> some kind of vacuum
> to sniff the scent of gold.
>
> > Mom tells me: Last year
> > he lost his wife to cancer.
> > They were best friends,
> > married forty years.
>
> He walks the lonely beach
> in an ugly Hawaiian shirt,

eyes shut, concentrating,
listening for the sound
of somebody else's
lost treasure.

Good luck with your poetry!

Mysteriously,

Ralph Fletcher

Playing with Fire

You said you
loved me
that afternoon
behind the woodpile
but when your father
collapsed at work
and died
without a hint
without a goodbye
your face
got all blurry gray
and I knew enough
to stay away.

All winter your ma
burned the wood
he had stacked
in the garage
to keep you warm
the wood so dry it
burned without smoke
until all the wood
was gone.

You said you
loved me
but when
I saw your face
I understood
we were just
playing
with that word.

DOUGLAS FLORIAN

Dear Young Poet,

Children often ask me, "When did you start to write poetry?" The answer may surprise you. I didn't write much poetry until about seven years ago. While in a flea market I bought a book called *Oh, That's Ridiculous!* It was edited by William Cole and had funny nineteenth-century children's rhymes as well as hilarious poems by more recent writers such as Ogden Nash, Spike Milligan, Shel Silverstein, and Laura Richards. I laughed so much that I decided then and there that I would try my hand at poetry.

That summer I wrote about 300 poems and sent them off to a publisher. Only about twenty of them ever got published, but that's the point. When you first start writing you have to do a lot of it before you get good at it. You have to get the hang of it.

Another bit of advice I would offer is to study your subject. Before I wrote my book *insectlopedia* I got my hands on as many insect books as possible. I studied field guides and hundreds of photographs. I stopped by the Museum of Natural History in New York City. I even interviewed a few mosquitoes (they really got under my skin with their infectious humor). From that research I learned a great deal about insects. For example, I discovered that whirligig beetles swim in circles on the surface of water. So naturally I wrote my poem in the shape of a circle. I also learned that termites in Africa build huge mounds above and below the ground. I shaped that poem like a tall thin termite mound. So do your research before you write your poem. Delve into nature and you'll find an endless supply of information to use.

How else can you write better poems? You might try by breaking a few rules. That's what e. e. cummings did when he created poems entirely in lower case letters. He felt that his poetry was more fresh and spontaneous that way. In poetry you can spell words wrong, use poor grammar, print words upside down, or even invent new words. That's called poetic license.

For example, you could call a howling wolf a "wooooolf." You might write about a "woodpeckpeck-pecker." How about a "smellephant"? In my book *Laugh-eteria*, I used my poetic license so much I almost got it suspended! There's one poem that's so bad it seems to fall off the page. My "do-it-yourself" poem has blanks to fill in because I was too lazy to finish it; *you* have to fill in the blanks. There's even a test poem before the title page.

Remember, in poetry, the only rule is that Poetry Rules!

All the beast,

Douglas Florian

Bad Poem

This poem is so bad
It belongs in the zoo.
It should jump in a lake
Or come down with the flu.
It should get itself lost
Or crawl into a cage.
This poem is so bad
It should

      fall

         off

            the

               page.

The Whirligig Beetles

We whirl,
we twirl,
we skate,
we glide.
Upon a pond or lake we ride.
We swim in circles like little toys,
without the windup keys or noise.

ADAM FORD

✄

To the young poet reading this book,

My advice to you if you are serious about writing poetry can be summed up in two words: *read* and *edit*.

Read poetry. Read a lot of it. Read as much of it as you can get your hands on. Try to work out what it is that other poets are trying to do. What structural techniques are they using? What kind of language are they using? Do you like what they're doing or not? Why does it work? Why doesn't it work? See if it's something you'd like to try yourself.

I'm really not one to talk about this, never having studied literature myself (my educational background is in science), but in the time that I've been writing, I've found that knowing the history of poetry helps you understand what poetry can and can't do. Reading other poets from a wide range of times and places can give you an idea of what poetry is capable of, and can help to inspire your own poems. When I'm suffering from writer's block, I find that reading other people's poetry gives me a kick in the pants that makes me want to write again.

Don't just limit yourself to reading poetry, though. Read novels, read comics, read newspapers and magazines, read everything. I've written poems inspired by the lyrics of my favorite bands, poems inspired by comics I read, poems inspired by articles in *New Scientist*, and poems inspired by stories in the newspaper. There's no telling where inspiration will come from, so open yourself up to as many experiences as possible, both by reading and by just being alive.

Edit your poems. It's always exciting when a poem tumbles straight from your head onto the page, but sometimes it still needs a little extra work. It's a rare poem whose first draft is as good as it could ever be. Put it aside for a couple of days and then come back to it. Does it still seem as good as it did when you wrote it? If it doesn't, try changing it. See if you can find any words that don't work so well and try to think of what words would work better in their place. See if you've used any clichés and try to express them in a different way. Poetry is as much about the structure of the words and the kind of words you use as it is about the content of the poem, so take your time. Let the poem mature. Poke it. Prod it. See if it stands up to your critical scrutiny. If it doesn't, try to work out *why* it doesn't and then change things. Sometimes it can help to get an outside opinion. Sometimes you can be too close to make an unbiased judgment on the quality of your writing, and at those times even just talking about the poem with someone else can get you thinking in a way that helps you come up with a solution to your problem.

I can't stress strongly enough the importance of revising your work. I've worked on a couple of poetry journals over the years, and I've seen a lot of poems that are pretty good, but which are also obviously unedited first drafts. There might be one or two really good lines or images in the poem, but if there's stuff in there that's less than great, it can spoil the effect of the good parts of the poem. With a little time taken and a little critical assessment, ordinary poems can become quite extraordinary. It's well worth the effort.

That's about all I have to say on the matter. Good luck with your poetry. Keep at it. Keep reading, keep editing, but above all, *keep writing*.

Smile

I was hypnotized
by a smile
at the tram stop.

This girl was kissing
this boy
and she was smiling.

She was smiling
even when she was
kissing him.

I couldn't see his face —
he was turned away
from me,

but I could see her.
I could see her smile.
And her smile

made me smile
as I hunkered down in my coat,
put my shoulders up

against the wind
and pretended that
I wasn't looking.

✂

When I was about ten years old,

I transformed my old backyard playhouse into a laboratory.
I had shelves filled with test tubes, scales, rocks I admired —
even pans of moss I'd haul home from the mountains —
because I loved the way they smelled of the forest.

I had a microscope and looked at everything I could
find. That's probably why I still remember those pans of
moss — because I studied them so closely. One kind was
covered with bursts of tiny stars; another had stalks of slen-
der gray flutes no larger than a letter *f* on this page.

I conducted countless experiments in my laboratory
and recorded my results in notebooks. I experimented with
germination by soaking different kinds of seeds and measur-
ing how long it took them to sprout. In the end, however,
what truly amazed me (and still does!) was the fact that
something small and dry and hard had a mysterious green
life tucked inside of it.

I'm the same way today. I still feel that same sense of
joy at discovery. I have questions about everything. The
world fascinates and astonishes me; I am often filled with
wonder.

My scientific notebook is now a writer's notebook. Instead of the results of scientific experiments, I record personal feelings, experiences, even the odd snippets of dreams I sometimes remember in the morning. I write about how it felt to be the only one in the choir to sing off key. About monkey wrenches, moose, and abandoned cabins in Colorado. My joy at seeing the *exact* moment a baby hummingbird left the nest and flew for the very first time.

I've always liked watching clouds and imagining what each cloud resembles. A panther? An iguana? Then, one day I suddenly noticed the images in the spaces *between* the clouds. My poem "The Blue Between" reminds me how I can look at something every day of my life and then, one day — "out of the blue" — I'll suddenly notice something I've never seen before.

Poetry is like that: being startled when you suddenly see the world differently. I've learned that the best surprises — the most astonishing discoveries — are all around me. I only have to stop and look carefully. Ideas for poems come to me when I pay attention to the world. When I truly *see* how a hawk cups the sky under its wings. When I notice how my little dog fits perfectly inside the sunny spot on the carpet. When I see a maple seed flutter by my kitchen window and I wonder: Where is it going?

These moments of discovery are when a poem will tap me on the shoulder. The same thing will happen for you. Listen to the questions in your mind. Don't take anything for granted. Let yourself be excited. Discover what astonishes you. When you feel strongly and deeply about something, you'll know. That's when your poem will find you.

Kristine O'Connell George

Maple Shoot in the Pumpkin Patch

Remember me?
I helicoptered past
your kitchen window last fall,
then hovered over the pumpkin patch.

I had traveled far on the wind that day,
spinning the whole entire way.
I really hadn't planned to stay,

only wanted to look around,
lay my dizziness down,
rest a moment on the ground.

No wind came to carry me aloft,
the dirt was sweet and soft—
I guess
I must
have
dozed
off. . . .

The Blue Between

Everyone watches clouds,
naming creatures they've seen.
I see sky differently,
I see the blue between —

>The blue woman tugging
>her stubborn cloud across the sky.
>The blue giraffe stretching
>to nibble a cloud floating by.
>A pod of dancing dolphins,
>cloud oceans, cargo ships,
>a boy twirling his cloud
>around a thin blue fingertip.

In those smooth wide places,
I see a different scene.
In those cloudless spaces,
I see the blue between.

NIKKI GRIMES

Dear Poet,

Imagery. Mastery. Honesty. As a poet, these are my watch-
words. Poetry calls for fresh imagery that rattles the senses
and carries the imagination to places it has never gone
before. A poem doesn't have to be smooth or delicious,
musically inviting or visually stunning, but when it rises
to that level, the poem can make the reader say "Wow!"
and I love that. Mastery refers to knowledge of the English
language. A poet is only as sharp as his tools, and a word-
smith with a limited vocabulary is bound to be dull.

    The third element is honesty. I'm talking here about
emotional honesty. If you're going to invest time in writing
something, especially poetry, which is such a pure form,
respect yourself and the reader enough to be honest. If
a subject frightens you or breaks your heart, show it. If it
makes you angry, let your poem shout. The same goes for
sweeter emotions. If, for instance, you're writing about
someone you feel compassion for, don't hide those feelings
behind tough-guy words or images. Bring your true self to
the page. Your honesty just might speak to and encourage
the reader who has experienced the same feelings, but was
unable to express them. I'm always moved by poems that

speak to the heart—which is why, as a writer, I tend to go for the emotional jugular.

Of course, there are books that can teach you about rhyme and meter, and it is certainly important to understand that good poetry requires a fair amount of revision. Scratch that. Good poetry requires a *great deal* of revision! Most of my poems go through ten drafts, minimum. (Groan.) That said, if you don't write honestly, no one will care what your poem has to say, no matter how cleverly written or technically competent it is.

Nikki Grimes

Sweethearts Dance

He pulls her close
    She strokes his face
Their thoughts fly to
    Their starting place

The Sweethearts Dance
    The day they met
He still remembers
    She can't forget

The music plays
    Just like before
The graying sweethearts
    Young once more
Whirl and dance
    Across the floor

Dear Poets,

To revise is a poet's life. To see and then to see again is what
a poet's life is all about. I revise my poems not for the sake
of revising, but to clarify what I see with my eyes and what's
in my heart.

One revision strategy that I've asked young poets to try
is what I call "the two-column poem." I divide my paper in
half, draw a line down the middle of the page, and in the
right column I briefly describe something that I see, either in
my mind's eye or in actuality, using the first words that come
to mind or "ordinary words." Then, I take a second and perhaps deeper look at what I've been looking at and describe it
more precisely in the left column. For example, if I describe a
pine tree outside my window as "green," I'll need to look at
it again because there are dozens of kinds of greens. I might
ask myself: Is the color green like the yellowish green of a
weeping willow tree in the spring; or is it the green of jade;
or the green of the sky before a storm? Each of these greens
is different in quality and will determine how the reader will
see my image of the pine tree.

When I write my poems, I'll need to re-see like this
sometimes five or six times before I get it right. It sounds like

a lot of work, and sometimes it feels like that but mostly, the reward is worth it because when I measure what I have written on paper with what's in my heart, they match — and I've created a poem.

Best poetry wishes,

Georgia Heard

Dragonfly

It skims the pond's surface,
searching for gnats, mosquitoes, and flies.
Outspread wings blur with speed.
It touches down
and stops to sun itself on the dock.
Wings flicker and still:
stained-glass windows
with sun shining through.

Dear Young Poet,

Always go back to things. They help you find out how you feel. Remember the locker door slamming at lunchtime? The SOLD sign on your front lawn when you finally realized you were moving? The green sweatshirt worn by the boy you had a crush on — or the tooth you lost at age six when you were running home from school?

Recently, when I went to help my parents move out of the house I grew up in, I came across a little wooden box in the attic. It contained six baby teeth. Suddenly I remembered saving them up for the tooth fairy so I could get a big cash return. Funny that I never did it. Was it some kind of savings account? Was I trying to save my childhood? Was I afraid of the pain of growing up? Memories mean nothing unless we go back to the baby teeth, the kitchen smelling of pot roast, your father's face darkening the day your dog died, the color of your best friend's bedspread. *Things* are the stuff of poems.

Even a wrinkle in a piece of paper can be the beginning of a poem! I started a poem once because I folded a letter from my sister right before I turned off the light to go to sleep. I did turn off the light, but not for long. I had to get up and write the line that came to me: "Now, dear sister, it is you who rescues me from the creases." That line ended up in the middle of the poem I eventually wrote, but it was the folded letter, the crease, that opened the door.

Even now, as I write this letter to you, a small spider is running across my laptop and up to my blue metal lamp. She's spinning silk from the screen to my keyboard, from my lamp to the desk, crisscrossing and swinging down again. Her work is the poet's work: making connections from thing to thing. I shall start a new poem for the spider. "She pulls her string from word to word. . . ."

Now you go do it, too.

In celebration of Things,

Christine Hemp

Connecting Cord

Launched on the NASA Submillimeter
Wave Astronomy Satellite Sent to Record
the Birth of Stars. December 5, 1998

When a child is waiting

to be born, light shines

inside. No one

but the mother knows

what trembles there.

She's the blanket, the safe

cloud, hiding her pinpoint

of glittery possibility.

Far beyond our monthly

tides and willful moon,

light years cut a path

to other embryos.

Clouds collapse, distant

swarms of gases swirl

through invisible infrared.

Sometime when you're

in the bathtub or driving

down the freeway, look up.

Turn away from grief

and your body which is fading

fast. Behind your reflection
in the water or the rearview
mirror, a star is asking
to be born. Feel

the ache in your forearms
when you pass a lifeless cat
along the road? The gash in your
heart when your lover leaves?

These are but the birth
pangs of a distant body
also yours. Waves of *becoming*
move out from wrinkled

sheets of time and space.
Heaven herself lets out a cry.
Transformation makes us writhe.
But when the crisis passes,

a new light sings: Fiery child,
sparking us to see a bigger
flame. Oh, and it's
burning, burning, burning!

Planet Earth, 1998

A *few thoughts:*

1. For a start, don't rhyme. We don't talk in rhyme—why should we write that way?
2. Write the way you talk. Think of the tone of the voice in your poem. Is it the way you speak?
3. Write about what you know. Sports. Friends. Parents. Teachers. Pets. Teachers' pets!
4. When you've written your poem, stand up and say it aloud. Work on how it sounds as well as how it reads. After all, poetry is about words—both spoken and written.
5. Good luck.

Seeing the World

Every month or so,
when my brother and I
are bored with backyard games
and television, Dad says
"It's time to see the world."

So we climb the ladder to our attic,

push the window open,

and carefully, carefully,

scramble onto the roof.

We hang on tight as we scale the heights

to the very top.

We sit with our backs to the chimney

and see the world.

The birds flying

        below us.

The trees swaying in the wind

              below us.

Our cubbyhouse, meters

          below us.

The distant city

        below us.

And then Dad, my brother, and I lie back

look up and watch

the clouds and sky

and dream

we're flying

we're flying.

In summer

with the sun and a gentle breeze

and not a sound anywhere

I'm sure I never want to land.

MARY ANN HOBERMAN

Dear Young Poet,

From as far back as I can remember, I always wanted to be a writer. Growing up, I never even considered any other calling. But of course I was writing long before I grew up. And before I could even print, let alone "write," before I started kindergarten, I was making up poems and stories and repeating them to myself or my little brother or my imaginary playmate, Billy. So it seems to me that I have *always* been a writer.

I think of our English language as a vast treasury, free for the taking. I marvel that our forebears created this subtle and supple instrument, equally adapted to communicating the most routine transactions and the most inspired flights of imagination. Feeling this way about words, I approach them as unique individuals, each with its own family history, its own color and rhythm and sound, speaking to us out of the past, connecting us with our own pasts, trailing multiple meanings, many of them subliminal but there to be unearthed and made use of by the poet, the lover of language.

If you look at language in this way, then the writer's calling becomes a noble one. Each time you discover the perfect word for your purpose, each time you shape a fine sentence, each time you awaken a reader's imagination, you will feel fulfilled. Here is the way John Updike, a gifted contemporary writer, once expressed it:

> My first thought about art, as a child, was that the artist brings something into the world that didn't exist before, and that [the artist] does it without destroying anything else. . . . That still seems to me its central magic, its core of joy.

I wish you a wonderful lifetime of writing.

Mary Ann Hoberman

May Fly

Think how fast a year flies by
A month flies by
A week flies by
Think how fast a day flies by
A May fly's life lasts but a day
A single day
To live and die
A single day
How fast it goes
The day
The May fly
Both of those.
A May fly flies a single day
The daylight dies and darkness grows
A single day
How fast it flies
A May fly's life
How fast it goes.

Pick Up Your Room

Pick up your room, my mother says
    (She says it every day);
My room's too heavy to pick up
    (That's what I always say).

Drink up your milk, she says to me,
    Don't bubble like a clown;
Of course she knows I'll answer that
    I'd rather drink it down.

And when she says at eight o'clock,
    You must go right to bed,
We both repeat my answer:
    Why not go left instead?

LEE BENNETT HOPKINS

Dear Poet,

Do you want
to write a poem?

Forget it . . .
until
you have
rewritten it.

Make your poem
stronger
by
not
writing a poem

but
rewriting it
and
rewriting it
and
rewriting it

until —

what you
have
is
a poem
like
no
other
poet
has
ever
written —

or

rewritten —

before!

CD a Poem

CD a poem.
Revolve it around.
Hear its bouncy rhythm
blare, blast, pound.

Let it clang,
boom,
rumble through
a city
farm
or
town.

Listen to it
rattle,
thunder —

but
never
turn
the volume
down.

Subways Are People

Subways are people—

    People standing
    People sitting
    People swaying to and fro
    Some in suits
    Some in tatters
    People I will never know.

    Some with glasses
    Some without
    Boy with smile
    Girl with frown

    People dashing
    Steel flashing
    Up and down and 'round the town.

Subways are people—

    People old
    People new
    People always on the go
    Racing, running, rushing people
    People I will never know.

ANDREW HUDGINS

&

Dear Young Writer,

The only people who ever become writers are readers. I read all the time. That doesn't make me special. Every writer I know reads all the time. The greatest place to do a little extra reading is the bathroom. Some people like to keep a book of jokes or cartoons on the back of the toilet. Not me. Poems are great bathroom reading. They're short and they each contain a whole thought, so you can finish two things at one time, if you know what I mean. Over two years, I read *The Collected Poems of Thomas Hardy* from beginning to end in my bathroom. It beats staring at the grout lines between the tile.

If you have a novel near your toilet, you'll finish your body business but not your reading business while you're in the bathroom — and unless you have a terrific memory, you'll keep forgetting the story. But if you're reading poetry, you can finish your body business and your poem business at the same time. Most of Thomas Hardy, Emily Dickinson, A. E. Housman, and E. A. Robinson's poems are the perfect size for quick reading. So are Shakespeare's sonnets. And in the Bible — the Psalms, Proverbs, and Ecclesiastes are great to drop into for a few moments. And, hey, I think my poems would make terrific bathroom reading.

But the bathroom is just one of the places I read poetry. I always have a book of poems by my bed to read before I go to sleep. I keep another book on the end table in the living room to dip into when TV gets too stupid for me to stand for another minute. There's always a book tossed in the back seat of the car so I'll have something to read if I get stuck waiting for my wife to come out of the bank or the post office. And ever since I was stranded in the Abilene airport for six hours with nothing to read, I never, ever go out of the house without at least two books in my backpack. Even if I don't read them — and I do — the extra weight on my back makes me stronger.

Andrew Hudgins

Grandmother's Spit

To wipe the sleep grains from my eyes or rub
a food smudge from my cheek, Grandmother'd lick
her rough right thumb and order me, *Come here.*
She'd clutch my arm and hold me near her face
while, with that spit-damp thumb, she scrubbed the spot.
I struggled like a kitten being licked,
then leaned into the touch, again catlike,
helping that fierce thumb scour loose the dirt.
It smelled, her spit, of lipstick and tobacco—
breath-warm, enveloping. She'd hold me at arm's length,
peer hard into my face, and state, *You're clean.*
When she let go, I'd crouch behind the door
and, with my own spit, rub the clean spot raw.

BOBBI KATZ

Dear Young Poet,

Some people think that they need to be swept away by some
strong emotion to write a good poem. Of course, it's great
when an experience moves you to such joy, sadness, anger,
or excitement that your pencil can hardly wait to capture it
on paper. And all of us love those poems that come rushing
out through our fingertips with the energy of a sudden
spring shower. They need so little fixing. It's as if we're just
the conduit—the hot wire. Yet I suspect that waiting for
those times of inspiration, depending on some energy surge,
can't begin to give you the same skills and satisfactions—
the same everyday joy—that acquiring the tools and practicing the craft of poetry can give you. When I visit schools, I'm
always surprised by the most commonly asked question:
Where do you get ideas? Ideas? I have *too* many of them!
There are so many poems, stories, and books that I'd like to
write that I'd need about thirty-three lifetimes to get halfway
through my list.

What possible advantage could an old crone like me
have over young people like you who have so much more
energy? I think the answer is my habits. So here come some
tips: You don't need a camera to take snapshots with words.

Focus your attention and frame a scene by quietly observing and experiencing the world around you. Trust your five senses to lead you to ideas, which are everywhere, just waiting for you to connect with them. Remember: words are a poet's basic tools. Collect vocabulary. Eat your words! Explore the taste as well as the sound of words. Does a word hum to you? Does it invite you to play? Does it beg you to repeat it? To rhyme it? The more words you know, the easier it will be to find the lines to create the images you want and to carry them where you want them to go.

And last, but not least, be prepared to revise. And revise. And revise. Sometimes I let a poem rest overnight, a few days, or even a few months before the last revision.

Have fun!

Bobbi
Katz

When Granny Made My Lunch

I always dreaded those days,
those embarrassing days,
when Granny made my lunch.
Her signature, a bulging brown paper bag,
splotched with grease stains,
bullying in front of the breakfast milk
so there was no way I could avoid
taking it out of the refrigerator.
No way it could possibly be "forgotten."

Even in the quiet of the kitchen,
I could imagine how the brown bag
would broadcast itself
in the room where we hung our coats
and shelved our lunches,
the pungent smell of raw onion
and rendered chicken fat
getting louder and louder.
I could hear the wild rumpus of smells:
fortissimo by noon.

At Mt. St. Mary's
the day-students ate in the gym,
edging the basketball court in dark green jumpers
pulled over brown-stockinged calves,
eyeing each other's lunches,
ready to swap half an egg salad
for half a bologna.
How I envied those neat flat rectangles
on packaged white bread.
Predictable.
Perfect.

Granny's sandwiches were left whole.
She wasn't taking any chances
that I might make a bad deal
for peanut butter and jelly
from a stranger's house.
On Granny days I tried
to hide my sandwich,

but how?

Exotic.

Gigantic.

A brass band of a sandwich

clamoring for attention,

the chopped liver heaped

between uneven slabs of pumpernickel

or sliced brisket piled on ragged rye.

And always,

always

the raw onion:

a Jewish star

in this place of crosses

marking me as an outsider.

No matter that Granny gave me an apple

and an orange.

No matter that she gave me a love token:

a napkin tied with a snip of ribbon,

a purse full of almonds and raisins.

The raw onion betrayed me.

It made me different from the girls at Mt. St. Mary's

and sister to those girls—

those other girls—

girls I only knew from pictures—

foreign girls from Poland and Rumania—

their faces pale and frightened

and a Jewish star

sewn on their coats.

X. J. KENNEDY

Dear Brother or Sister Poet,

What's the best thing to write about? Many people will give
you an easy answer: write about something you know. That
advice can be helpful, especially if you're writing a story, or
a paper for school. A well-known American writer, Russell
Baker, has remembered how, as a kid, he had an awful time
writing any paper that would please his English teacher. At
last he gave up trying to please her and wrote about something he himself liked: eating spaghetti. To his surprise, his
teacher thought his paper was terrific.

But writing a poem isn't the same as writing a school
paper. (Unless, of course, your teacher assigns you to write a
poem — as lots of smart teachers do these days.) Poems,
unlike most book reports, are made out of feelings. So it
isn't enough just to write about what you know. You have
to find something you know that you deeply care about.

Asked one time by a student poet for ideas to write
about, poet Karl Shapiro replied, "Praise something!" In
other words, find something you love, and write a poem to
celebrate it. Who or what do you care about? A friend, a
relative, a pet, or maybe spaghetti? Then praise that subject
in a poem.

Because good poems arise out of strong feelings, the opposite advice will work too. You can write about something you despise. Jack Prelutsky has a memorable poem whose title (and first line) is "Homework! Oh, Homework." (The second line is "I hate you! You stink!")

Other feelings may rise in you. Do you feel like crying? Does something make you afraid? Get it down on paper. If something makes you laugh, tell us what's funny about it. (A word of warning here: if you write about why your best friend is ridiculous, you might not have that friend anymore.)

All around you, life is happening, ready and waiting for you to capture it in poems. Events at school, the doings of your family or friends, anything that happened to you in the past—a few minutes ago, or a few years. Maybe, at this very moment, someone or something you feel deeply about is in the room with you. Possibly ten poems are waiting for you to write them—here and now. Some of these things might seem so small and unimportant that you'll wonder, who would want to read about this? But in fact you can make another person want to read about it, about practically anything at all, if only it makes you *feel* enough, if only you can bring it alive for your reader in lively words.

One more suggestion. Feelings in poetry are what matter most, so if you find yourself feeling strongly about something you've never seen or experienced in person, go ahead and write about it anyway. Just imagine it. That's what Samuel Taylor Coleridge did in a wonderful poem called "Kubla Khan." That's what John Keats did in "Ode to a Nightingale" when he brought alive for us his dream of "magic casements, opening on the foam / Of perilous seas in faery lands forlorn."

Why not look up those famous poems with the aid of your teacher or librarian, and sample some really first-rate imagining? And keep on reading poetry. Roam around in books; find what really speaks to you. I'll make you a promise: The more you read, the better you'll write.

Good luck and have fun,

X.J. Kennedy

Who Clogged Up Our Schoolbell with Bubblegum?

Who clogged up our schoolbell with bubblegum?
Oh, who could have been such a fink?
The *clang clang* that woke us each morning
Is now a pathetic *tink tink*.

Who clogged up our schoolbell with bubblegum?
Who did it, the miserable skunk?
Whose sticky old snapper has clung to the clapper?
Now it strikes with a terrible *clunk*.

Who clogged up our schoolbell with bubblegum?
Who strangled its song with chewed string?
It must have been awful, the size of the jawful
That gummed up that old ding-a-ling.

Who clogged up our schoolbell with bubblegum?
Since then, we've had nothing but trouble,
For when Teach gives a pull on its rope to start school
Our bell blows a giant pink bubble.

KARLA KUSKIN

Dear You,

I am writing to you about writing. It is something we both do, but it is not something that I discuss with other people very often. Maybe that is because I do most of my writing and drawing when I am alone.

I am used to being by myself. I think some people are drawn to solitary arts to get away from other people. Maybe they come from big, noisy families and need time to think their own thoughts and put them down privately. On the other hand, there are those of us who grow up without many people around (I had no sisters or brothers), so being alone is a fact of life from very early on. Certainly we all have private thoughts that we want to remember. Those of us who are writers write them down. Painters paint them.

As an only child I talked to myself. I still do when no one else is present. Talking things out helps me to understand them. And writing is a kind of conversation with myself. It is also a way of keeping myself company. As I write, my thoughts get clearer. Before I could write, I would make up short poems and stories and my mother would write my words down. That encouraged me to make up more stories and poems. I'm still at it.

If you asked me what equipment I think a writer needs, my first answer would not be a computer. I think it is more important for a writer to have a good eye and a sharp ear. A writer, any artist, usually begins by paying close attention to the world. Of course, paying attention includes reading as much and as often as you can. Books are always introducing you to new people and ideas, and taking you to places you have never been.

Where do you get the idea for a poem?
Does it shake you awake?
Do you dream it asleep?
Or into your tiny tin head does it creep
and pop from your head when you are not aware
or leap from your pocket
or fall from your hair
or is it just suddenly silently there?

My guess is that our ideas are a combination of what is outside and inside each of our heads. That is why it is so important to pay attention to everything around you. Any detail can start you writing. For instance, you see the man across the street in that old blue overcoat? Was he once a pirate, or possibly, a baseball player? Watch his walk, wonder about him, let your imagination roam. And please let me read the story or poem you write about him when you have finished it.

Karla Kuskin

— ✦ —

From portal to portal
trudges the turtle.
It startles a toadstool
and treads through the myrtle.
It stops here and there
to speak to a stone.
The turtle's a mortal
who doesn't much chortle
from portal to portal
he turtles alone.

—✂—

Days that the wind takes over
blowing through the gardens
blowing birds out of the street trees
blowing cats around corners
blowing my hair out
blowing my heart apart
blowing high in my head
like the sea sound caught in a shell.
One child put her thin arms around the wind
—and they went off together.
Later the wind came back
—alone.

J. PATRICK LEWIS

Dear Young Poet,

Ignore, if you wish, all of these fractured bits of advice —
except for the first and last.

Book your eyes on a never-ending cruise: become a
lifelong reader.

Use your slow hand at writing poetry. What comes fast
and easy is invariably cheesy. (Like that sentence.)

As with food-chewing, revise each poem at least
thirty-two times. Or pretend you are "going down and
down./For the good turf. Digging," as the Nobel Laureate
Seamus Heaney put it.

Nothing succeeds like failure. Revel in it. You may take
a measure of pride if you can say, "I failed three times today,
and that was before lunch."

Fill up on verbs (fiber); go sparingly on adjectives and
adverbs (fat).

If you choose to rhyme, beware: the bar of excellence
rises considerably because it's so easy to write — yet so
painful to read — contrived rhymes.

Don't confuse free verse with a license to spill words
slapdash. Free verse also plays by rhythm's rules.

The Muse is not the type to whisper poems in your ear. Seek her out. Not long ago, thumbing through *The Guinness Book of World Records,* I came across a curious little item, which led to

First Parachute Wedding

Ann Hayward/Arno Rudolphi
World's Fair, New York City
August 25, 1940

Suspended there

Above the Fair,

A bride and groom

And love . . . in bloom.

The best man swayed

Beside the maid

Of honor who

Admired the view.

Humanity

Looked up to see

The strings of four

Musicians soar.

The preacher said,

"I do thee wed."

These high-flown words

Alarmed the birds.

The couple kissed

(But mostly missed)

Until they floundered
to the ground.

From skies above
They fell . . . in love.
Her wedding vow?
A simple "Wow!"

[Note: According to newspaper accounts, the minister, the married couple, the best man, the maid of honor, and four musicians all came down in parachutes.]

And after that poem appeared in my children's book *A Burst of Firsts*, I thought, why not a second collection of on-the-edge, "extreme poems"? A couple of modest examples:

Longest Time Stuck in an Elevator

Graham Coates
Brighton, England
Trapped in an elevator
For 62 hours
May 24–27, 1986

It is chilly, it is lonely
When you find yourself the only
Population in an elevator car.

It is quiet, it is scary
When you are the solitary
Population in an elevator car.

It is drafty, it is creepy
When you have become one sleepy
Population in an elevator car.

Three days later, what a tingle
When you learn you're not the single
Population in an elevator car!

Or,

Shortest Street in the World

Elgin Street, Bacup, England

Go take a walk
Down Elgin Street
Where people talk . . .
For seventeen feet.

"Good day!"
                    "Hello!"
Is all they say —
Then turn, and go
The other way.

The point, which is by now a cliché, is that poems are all
around you, from the remembered hills of childhood to
people-watching at the mall.

Book your eyes: read on.

GEORGE ELLA LYON

Dear Friend,

If you rearrange the letters in *word*, you can get *rowd*, which makes me think of *road* and *rowed*, path and labor. I expect you feel a calling to travel the word-road or you wouldn't be reading this.

How can you do it? Well, I wish there were a number you could call for a map of the route, but that's not possible. Being part of your life, your word-road is under constant construction. No one can give you a map, but I hope I can offer some things that will be helpful as you find your own way.

First of all, as writer Flannery O'Connor said, "Art is the habit of the artist." Writing is a practice, not something you just do in a burst of energy now and then. Most people know if you want to be on the swim team, you don't jump in the water for the first time at tryouts. And, if you make the team, you don't swim only in meets. No, you practice, practice, practice. It's the same thing if you want to sing with a band or play in a chess tournament. Working at your dream becomes part of your every day life.

A great practice place is your journal. Cultivate the habit of writing in it every day—dreams, observations, memories, things people say — whatever catches your heart. Just doing this will make you more responsive. And it will make you more fluent in translating from the outside world to the written page.

But you don't need to confine your journal to words. You can draw, paint, paste in pictures, tickets, leaves, fabric, notes from friends — anything that helps capture the texture of your life. For me, the journal is a friend, a companion on the way. And sometimes poems jump right out of it!

My second piece of advice is to read all you can, including books about writers' lives, so you can see there are as many ways of being a writer as there are people writing. You're not alone, though you may sometimes feel like it. There are lots of other folks out there looking for the word-road. Try to find someone in your school or neighborhood who shares this interest. It's great to have someone to swap poems with.

And finally, don't confuse getting published with writing. Getting published is wonderful, of course, but it's not the point. The point is to get what's in your heart and head on paper and then shape it in a way that satisfies you and speaks to others. There are lots of ways to share your work with the world. You can read it aloud or give it to someone. You can make your own book, by hand or via computer and copier. You can send it in a letter to a friend. Formal publication, if it comes, will probably take a long time. Don't let that stop you from writing. Be tough. Have fun.

May the ink be with you!

George Ella Lyon

Where I'm From

I am from clothespins,
from Clorox and carbon-tetrachloride,
I am from the dirt under the back porch.
(Black, glistening,
it tasted like beets.)
I am from the forsythia bush
the Dutch elm
whose long-gone limbs I remember
as if they were my own.

I'm from fudge and eyeglasses,
    from Imogene and Alafair.
I'm from the know-it-alls
    and the pass-it-ons,
from Perk up! and Pipe down!
I'm from He restoreth my soul
    with a cottonball lamb
    and ten verses I can say myself.

I'm from Artemus and Billie's Branch,
fried corn and strong coffee.
From the finger my grandfather lost
    to the auger,
the eye my father shut to keep his sight.

Under my bed was a dress box
spilling old pictures,
a sift of lost faces
to drift beneath my dreams.
I am from those moments—
snapped before I budded—
leaf-fall from the family tree.

LILIAN MOORE

When I was a child

growing up in New York City, the place I loved most was the
neighborhood library, where I feasted on endless stories. So
it seemed natural that when I began to write for children, I
wrote stories. The only poetry I wrote were verses about very
little children like my own young son.

One day an editor asked me if these verses could make
a book. As I looked them over, something happened, like a
great unlocking. Instead of being interested in verses telling
how little children felt, I began to recover memories of my
own — how I felt the first time I saw the sun-dappled sea,
how it felt to breathe "dragon smoke" on the way to school
on a cold winter day, how haunting was the sound of a
foghorn in the bay at night.

So I wrote poems about these memories. It was a special pleasure to revisit experiences in this new way. And the
poems kept coming, as if I now had the power to see and to
hear more acutely.

Years later I moved to a farm in the country. Here, too,
everything clamored to become a poem. But of course
poems are everywhere once they start in your head. That's
actually the way my poems do start. I hear in my head the

line and the rhythm a poem will take. Sometimes the line gets stuck there.

Once, after a long dry spell on the farm, I wrote the first line of a poem: "Roots have forgotten the taste of rain." I liked it, but I couldn't move forward into a poem. A poet friend, to whom I mentioned my frustration, suggested that I "back into the line." That's just what I did. It became the last line in the poem "Dry Spell."

I tend to write poems slowly because I enjoy seeking the right word and revising until I think I have it. For almost every poem I have written over the years there has probably been a wastebasket filled with rough drafts. Most of all, I want a poem to say what I really felt or saw or heard—that is, to be true.

Lilian Moore

Waterfall

Winter breathed on the
waterfall   stilled it
left ragged icicles
hanging from the rocks.

Through short dark days and
long dark nights
we missed the chatter,
the rollicking spill.

Warm winds came   uncurling
leaves on maple trees,
forsythia glowed
like lights turned on.

Still
the waterfall
hung silent
in tattered ice.

We waited.

We heard it
today   the joyous rush,
saw water leaping again
over rocks,

spraying sunlight,
announcing
the news:
"*Now* it's spring!"

Poets Go Wishing

Poets go fishing
with buckets
of words,
fishing
and wishing.

Using a line
that's loose or
tight
(Maybe this time
a rhyme is right.)

Unreeling
unreeling
the words till they
match
the feeling the poet is
trying to
catch.

LILLIAN MORRISON

Dear Young Poet,

Welcome to poetry. Writing poems has enhanced my life
and will yours for as long as you continue to write. Why?
Because, for one thing, as a poet, all your senses are alert.
You become a keen noticer of people, things, and experiences. You are aware of taste, touch, smells, colors, shapes,
sounds, and certainly feelings, your own and other people's.
Keeping your eyes and ears and heart open as you write, little by little, you get to see better, hear better, and know and
understand more about yourself and the world around you.
Poetry makes you smart.

Thoughts and pictures come to your mind, but unlike
most people, you do not let them slip by as unimportant.
You hang on to those you want to capture and put them in
poems to share with others. Your raw materials, of course, are
words, which you group together in a shape or rhythmical
structure—your poem. Words are endlessly fascinating. A
string of them can make a music all its own. It doesn't have
to be sublime. When I was four years old, "Marguerite, go
wash your feet, the Board of Health's across the street" had
the power to fill me with delight. Play with words. Enjoy
their sounds, shapes, meanings, and use them precisely.

Then there's rhythm and rhyme—a good part of my pleasure in that chant I heard as a child. Your poem's rhythm does not have to be very obvious. But whether you use rhyme and a regular beat or prefer the subtler cadence of free verse, a rhythm is always there. We live in a rhythmical universe, from the dance of atoms and our own heartbeats to the ocean tides and the movements of the planets. When I write, sometimes I feel in touch with that universal rhythm. It's an exciting feeling.

Your impressions and responses are going to be somewhat different from anyone else's. That makes them interesting. Although you have much in common with other people, there is nobody exactly like you. Often what you see and sense will remind you of something similar. A good eye for resemblances, especially unexpected ones, is a great asset. The resemblances in my poem "The Boxing Match" happen to come from sports, probably because I am a sports fan. There are many other kinds of poems: funny poems, those which explore a high moment, a mood, a memory, a happening, and there are many other techniques poets use for effect, as you will discover.

Meanwhile, some final advice. Use a notebook for your ideas, dreams, and lines and phrases you want to remember. When you need inspiration, your notebook can get you started again. Express your true feelings, not what you think you ought to feel. Read lots of good poetry—out loud or aloud in your head. And have fun.

So here's to you. Here's to seeing the world freshly with your own eyes and adding your bit to the sum of created things in it.

Lillian Morrison

The Boxing Match

Two bushes have come to blows.
The wind is egging them on.
Their shadows are boxing here on the rug
In a broad strip of sun.

Wham, wham, they bob and weave,
Then abruptly the battle is done.
The wind has rushed to another arena.
Nobody hurt. Nobody won.

Tugboat at Daybreak

The necklace of the bridge
is already dimmed for morning
but a tug in a tiara
glides slowly up the river,
a jewel of the dawn,
still festooned in light.

The river seems to slumber
quiet in its bed,
as silently the tugboat,
a ghostlike apparition,
moves twinkling up the river
and disappears from sight.

NAOMI SHIHAB NYE

To My Dear Writing Friends,

I know *revision* may sound like an ugly word to you. I didn't love it when I was in school. If a teacher told me to *revise*, I thought that meant my writing was a broken-down car that needed to go to the repair shop. I felt insulted. I didn't realize the teacher was saying, "Make it shine. It's worth it."

Now I see *revision* as a beautiful word of hope. It's a new vision of something. It means you don't have to be perfect the first time. What a relief!

In first drafts, you may write phrases and fragments, then connect and develop them later into something larger like a poem. Or you may overwrite first—lavishly, loosely— and pare it down later. Most of us work both ways, depending on moods and the moment.

The possibilities of revision take away pressure, which helps the whole process. Who needs stress?

Many students say they don't like to revise because they don't want to tamper with their first pure, honest expression. But why should your second (or fourth) consideration of something be less genuine than your first? You're still you! Now that you've had time to think a bit more, you may find it very helpful to rearrange words or specify or animate a thought or detail.

Revision may be as small as a single, crucial word change. I replaced the word "nowhere" with "everywhere" in the last stanza of a poem and that one difference changed everything.

Or a revision may be dramatic. Once an editor suggested I cut the first thirty lines of a poem. "Then you'll really have something," he said. But the poem only had thirty-six lines! At first I thought he was ridiculous. But the more I ruminated, the more I could see he was right. The first thirty lines were a preface to the real poem.

I love the little arrows that invite more words into a line. And what a pleasure it is, striking extra or weaker ones out! *Adios, you unnecessary "very"! Farewell, cluttery "the"!*

A line or phrase grows lean and strong before our eyes. Penciled *x*'s! Punched delete buttons! (Make sure you keep copies of drafts. Save, save, save.)

It's a good idea to leave time (an hour, a day, a week, whatever) between writing a first draft and revising it. That space and distance help you see your work with a fresher eye. Also, I STRONGLY advise that you read your work out loud to yourself as you revise it. No need to feel foolish. The best writers do this, and it will help you more than anything else.

Now and then, something you write comes out wonderfully well in a first draft. Changes aren't necessary. The more you write, the more this may happen. But the delicious gift of revision is that *it doesn't have to happen all the time.*

Love,

Naomi Shihab Nye

How do I know when a poem is finished?

When you quietly close
the door to a room
the room is not finished.

It is resting. Temporarily.
Glad to be without
you for a while.

Now it has time to gather
its balls of gray dust,
to pitch them from corner to corner.

Now it seeps back into itself,
unruffled and proud.
Outlines grow firmer.

When you return,
you might move the stack of books,
freshen the water in the vase.

I think you could keep doing this
forever. But the blue chair looks best
with the red pillow. So you might as well

leave it that way.

Every Cat Had a Story

The yellow one from the bakery
smelled like a cream puff—
she followed us home.
We buried our faces
in her sweet fur.

One cat hid her head
while I practiced violin.
But she came out for piano.
At night she played sonatas
on my quilt.

One cat built a secret nest
in my socks.

One sat in the window
staring up the street all day
while we were at school.

One cat loved
the radio dial.

One cat almost
smiled.

TOM POW

Dear Young Poet,

Perhaps you have already had to answer the common question, "Why do you write?" If not, perhaps we can answer it together.

There are, of course, an infinite number of reasons why we write—and go on writing—poems. Here are five of them:

- Your pet has died.
- Your team has won a trophy.
- It's snowing.
- The *Titanic* has just sunk.
- You're in love.

It's surely not hard to imagine that on each of these occasions you would want to put your feelings into words as clearly as you could—and as memorably.

When we write a letter to someone to tell them we love them, we want to make sure we are expressing our true and possibly complex feelings, but we also want the person to remember our letter—which is why we may think of writing a poem. A poem gives us access to a whole bag of tricks—imagery, rhythm, rhyme, shape, compression—that will make our words (hopefully) stick in the mind.

I think that in the special circumstances of an out-standing event or a very emotional one, it is the most natural response in the world to write a poem. What makes someone a poet, or at least someone for whom poetry will be an important part of life, is that he or she will be interested in expressing the whole range of human emotion — from the happiest to the saddest and all the gray areas in between. He will also be someone who gets a kick out of language, a buzz from exploring the bag of tricks.

Of course, we all have areas of experience that interest us more than others. I suppose mine can most easily be described as *Landscape* and *Memory*. In his *Letters to a Young Poet* (one of which I always carry within the covers of my notebook), the German poet Rilke says, "Even if you were in a prison whose walls allowed none of the sounds of the world to reach your senses — would you not still have always your childhood, that precious royal richness, that treasure house of memories?" And although I am far from my childhood now, it is surprising how accessible the "treasure house of memories" can still be.

My poem "The Polar Bear" twins two memories — one a very recent one and the other again from childhood. The poem is, I suppose, a rather belated appreciation of how unhappy caged animals can be and how insensitive children can be to them. But it fails as a poem if it can't make the reader see the wonderful bear. For my favorite poets are those who can make us see: I think of the Scottish poet Norman MacCaig, of Seamus Heaney, and of Elizabeth Bishop. In "The Polar Bear," I have tried to convince the reader that what drew us, and many others, to a huge tank in Central Park Zoo, lived in the world of the senses we all inhabit. Although many of my poems focus on experiences that I have carried around for years and years before I was able to give them shape, "The Polar Bear" describes something I saw only last summer. Still, I hope my poems, no matter where they come from, capture experiences as freshly as if they had happened only yesterday.

Tom C. Pow

The Polar Bear

I remember the polar bears
of my childhood. How they stood
alone on their worn rocks and stared
over the gray water and the wood
that divided us. How they rocked
from paw to paw; their heads reined low,
going to and fro. How we mocked
them!—mimicking their stagnant show,
as if it were we who controlled
their rhythms. In similar ways,
through the monkey house, we patrolled
with a riot of scratchings; we lay
before the stick-still crocodile
and the glare of its onyx eye.
Animals were there to be riled—
and if now you ask me why,

I'd say, because we craved something
from them: the rooted elephant
to rampage, to make its cage ring
with its power. We all showed scant
interest in surface beauty. Birds
of Paradise, tropical fish—
they were adjectives, not the words
we cared for; those that could unleash
pure meaning: *elephant, monkey,*
crocodile, bear.
Which goes some way
to explain how it was, a key
turned in me when we saw, at play
in Central Park Zoo, a ragged
avalanche of purest snow that
never shattered into the jagged
wedges of itself. But, as the black
prow of its nose hit the tank glass,
the smooth snow-block of its head turned
and it kicked against its white mass
with a giant paw. And I learned
what a pool of unhappiness
there has been—so many lives
blighted, so many tendencies
never unwrapped. Our hearts were hives
of joy as we looked from the bear
into our children's eyes; while ghosts
of other children, other bears,
loomed from the margins of the lost.

JACK PRELUTSKY

Hello Young Poet,

Would you like to write a funny poem? Here are three ways
to get you started:

1. **Exaggerate.** This is one of the easiest techniques. You can
    make almost anything funny if you stretch your imagina-
    tion and amplify your idea with silly and wild descrip-
    tions. This is a device I used in "Euphonica Jarre," from
    The New Kid on the Block.

    If you want to try this technique yourself, pretend you
    have a sister who likes to dance, but when she does, she
    looks very strange.

    Here are a couple of lines about a dancing sister—see
    what bizarre descriptions you can create:

    > My sister is a dancer and she loves to dance all day,
    > But when she dances it's the strangest thing to watch,
    > She looks like . . .

2. **Make the ordinary special.** One easy way to do this is to
    combine silly ideas with ordinary things you see around

you all the time. I created an outrageous combination when I wrote my poem "Rat for Lunch" (from *A Pizza the Size of the Sun*). We eat lunch every day, but what if your favorite meal is a rat!??!

See if you can concoct some funny dishes to eat. Let's say you have a wacky grandma who loves to make very "special" meals:

> My grandma cooked for us today
>
> We had so much to eat
>
> She started with . . .

3. **Absurd conclusion**. This technique may be a little bit harder, but if you use your imagination, you'll come up with some good ideas. In this poem you want an idea to keep escalating until it goes off the deep end.

   This is what I mean. Something happens. Then it happens again, only bigger (louder, funnier, etc.). Then it happens again and again until only some silly conclusion remains. That's how I constructed the poem "My Mother Made a Meatloaf" (from *Something Big Has Been Here*).

   Try it yourself. Here's one idea: maybe your baby brother or sister spills a glass of chocolate milk on the rug and the stain won't come out. First your dad uses a paper towel to wipe it up, but the spot won't go away. Next your dad uses the mop, but the spot still won't disappear. Then he rubs it with chicken grease, but no luck. This goes on until finally the spot is gone, but now the rug is completely destroyed!

   I've started the poem for you. Let's see if you can think of things to do to this rug that are crazier and crazier:

My baby brother dropped a glass of chocolate milk
  on Mama's new white rug.
When my father tried to clean it up nothing seemed
  to work.
First he used a paper towel, then he scrubbed it with
  a mop.
Then he . . .

My Final Writing Advice: Your ideas are more important than trying to make a perfect rhyming poem. Your poem should have a sense of rhythm — it should sound like a song and have a repeating beat like a soft drum tap. BUT YOU DON'T HAVE TO MAKE THE LINES RHYME!!! That takes lots of practice and right now, when you're just beginning to write poetry, it's more important to learn how to think creatively and how to arrange your ideas.

Your friend,

Euphonica Jarre

Euphonica Jarre has a voice that's bizarre
but Euphonica warbles all day,
as windowpanes shatter and chefs spoil the batter
and mannequins moan with dismay.

Mighty ships run aground at her horrible sound,
pretty pictures fall out of their frames,
trees drop off their branches,
rocks start avalanches,
and flower beds burst into flames.

When she opens her mouth, even eagles head south,
little fish truly wish they could drown,
the buzzards all hover, as tigers take cover,
and rats pack their bags and leave town.

Milk turns into butter and butterflies mutter
and bees look for something to sting,
pigs peel off their skins, a tornado begins
when Euphonica Jarre starts to sing.

LIZ ROSENBERG

To a Young Poet,

First of all, don't read my letter now. First read *Letters to a Young Poet* by Rainer Maria Rilke, who was a great poet, and a great letter writer to boot. But if it's out of the library, go ahead and read this letter.

What do young poets need to know? I am trying to remember what I wanted to know.

How to begin? How to get better? If you love poetry, that's a good start. If you have a favorite poet, maybe you could memorize a few poems by him/her, so you can carry them around whenever you need or want them. Certain poems—like favorite trees, or views or memories—become old friends over time. You have that company for the rest of your life. (One of my best poem friends is "Stopping by Woods on a Snowy Evening" by Robert Frost. Another is "Sometimes with One I Love" by Walt Whitman.)

For me, writing is like playing a wonderful game, the kind where you lose track of time and your father or mother has to stand out in the streets after dark, calling you to come home. Maybe you keep a journal—a good habit. (Though not in any way necessary. No "way" is necessary!) If you do like jotting down ideas, quotes, lines, scraps of poems, things people say, pick a book that's small enough to fit into whatever you carry around with you every day, and get in the habit of writing things down. Write letters. Learn how to write stories (poets need to do this, too!) and, of course, write your poems.

Let's say you write something you don't altogether love at first. Maybe there's something you forgot to say in the poem, or said the wrong way, or you just don't like the music of the poem. (Never forget the music of the poem! Poetry isn't prose chopped into shorter lines.) Put it aside for a few days—hide it from yourself. I tuck mine behind my typewriter, or lay it face down on my desk, or under a pile of other poems. When you look at it after a few days, or a week, or a few weeks, it will seem almost new to you, at least for the first minute that you glance at it. That's a good time to revise (which means: to look again, or see again) because you have what Buddhists like to call a "fresh mind."

A fresh mind is, in my opinion, the most wonderful thing a poet can possess—in life, and in writing. It means looking at things in a new way, clearly and unafraid. Revision is my favorite part of writing a poem—that and the first instant a poem strikes. They are the opposite ends of the same process: one is like lightning, the other more like a steady lamp. Both ways, I feel I am working toward the light— some image, idea or memory or story to tell.

If you feel confused and unsure about poetry, that's okay, too. There is no wrong way to come to poetry. As the poet Antonio Machado wrote, "There is no path. You make the path in going." All paths can be good: if you like to write funny poetry, or sad poetry, or rhyming poetry, long, narrative poetry, or little tiny jewel-like poems. As the Buddhist grocer once said, "All my groceries are best." Writing poetry is not a competition, not a race — it's a process. If you don't love the process, then find something else you *do* love!

But I hope poetry will give you great joy and comfort in your life, as it has given me.

Your friend,

Liz Rosenberg

The Christmas Cactus

All during the Christmas rush
I waited for the thing to come alive.
Eyed it while I gift wrapped scarves,
withered it with scorn as I threw
the green and silver bundles under the tree.
By New Year's
I vowed to be happy
living with just stems.

Then one day in February—
the worst month of the year,
making up in misery what it lacks in length—
the blooms shot out,
three ragged cerise bells that rang
their tardy Hallelujahs on the sill.
Late bloomers,
like the girls that shine
and shine at long last
at the spring dance
from their corner of the gym.

ALICE SCHERTLE

Whoever you are,
wherever you are,

there's a poem within arm's reach of you. Probably lots of poems, but at least one. Guaranteed. Are you in your room? At a taco drive-through? In a sleeping bag? In a tree? A poem is there.

Robert Frost once saw a mite crawling across his paper. He raised his pen to "stop it with a period of ink/when something strange about it made me think." That moment— poised to drown a microscopic bug with a drop of ink— grew into a thirty-three-line poem called "A Considerable Speck."

It was the thinking that did it. Thinking about the ordinary things around you makes you see them for what they are: poems. Whoever you are, wherever you are, there's a poem within reach — if you think about it. If you read to the end of his poem, you'll hear Frost (he could be a grouch) growling about poets who leave the thinking part out of the process.

If there's not a bug to be found scooting across your paper, all is not lost. Reach into your pocket. Take out what- ever's in there — a nickel, a movie ticket stub, a key, stuck- together jelly beans — they're all poems. Nothing in your pocket but a pinch of lint? Lint poem. You really came up empty handed? Perfect. Write about an empty pocket. The thing is to think about it, and because you have a mind wonderfully different from anyone else's mind, you'll write the poem no one else would have written.

I used to think that poems could be found only in "big" subjects like beauty, wonder, birth, death, love. Now I like to find the poems that lurk in unexpected places—on a slice of pepperoni pizza, perhaps, or floating down the gutter after a rain. I once found a pretty good poem in the ear of my cat. Oddly enough, I sometimes find the big subjects lurking somewhere within the little unexpected poems. I've written a lot of poems about animals. I never know what directions these poems will take, but I've noticed that a lot of my poems about animals have made me think about *human* nature. I've known a few people like the frog in the well who explains the world. If the frog in my poem ever makes it to the top, he might discover that there's a lot more world than the one-star view from the bottom of a well.

I've never been to the bottom of a well myself, fortunately. But a writer's imagination—anyone's imagination—is never farther away than the next thought. That's why there's no limit to the number of poems waiting for you to find them. There are times, of course, when it feels as if someone has snuck in and scooped up, vacuumed up, swept away every possible poem. Maybe, as in my poem "Writing Past Midnight," you stay up very late looking for them—nodding off, waking and writing. Then, suddenly, happily, there's the poem, right there in plain sight. And you reach out and put it on the page.

Alice Schertle

A Frog in a Well
Explains the World

The world is round
and deep
and cool.
The bottom of the world's
a pool
with just enough room
for a frog alone.
The walls of the world
are of stone on stone.
At the top of the world,
when I look up high,
I can see a star
in a little round sky.

Writing Past Midnight

insects drone . . . the night draws on . . .
I am writing a poem about a barn . . .

and my room is warm with the breath of horses
and dust from the loft runs in streams down the walls
and somewhere the sound
of sheep snoring softly
blends with the hum of computers
asleep in their stalls

bundled with bailing wire
stanzas
are stacked
to the ceiling

spiderwebs anchor the edge of my desk to the floor
a small gray verse runs squeaking down one of the rafters

just as the moon floats in through the double barn door

MARILYN SINGER

As far back
as I can remember,

I've always loved poetry—reading it and writing it. Here are
two poems I wrote when I was in first grade:

> When I was walking on the ocean floor,
>> there were many sights to adore.
> But one sight gave me a fright.
> It was a whale with a big long tail
>> that I simply drat.
> And I went so close that with its tail
>> it went spat, spat, spat.

> Rain, rain hitting my windowpane,
>> where does it come from?
> Some folks hate rain.
> Some children think it's lonesome.
> I know a little tale about rain,
>> when it went hitting and dripping
>>> down my windowpane.

The first poem has bad grammar and the second is a little corny, but I like them. They remind me that when I was a kid, I both studied things and imagined them. They show me that I let whales, rain, and a host of other creatures, characters, and natural forces tell me their tales.

Today, when I write poetry, I still study things. I look at the way one person or frog or foggy day is unique and also how it fits into the bigger picture; I try to see both the forest and the individual trees. Some of my poems are like snapshots—I write exactly what I see (or think I see) at a particular moment. Other poems of mine are fantasies. Sometimes I write about real people. Other times I make up characters. Some of those characters talk in rhyme. Many of them don't. But all of them speak poetry.

Why do I have animals and people speak poetry, when we know that in real life they don't? For me, poetry is what they're saying *inside*—their true thoughts and feelings. And it's not just *what* they'd say, but *how* they might say it. You know that some folks are more down-to-earth and have a plainer way of talking while others use fancier language. I think, if they could talk, some animals would speak in many different ways, as well. A turtle, for example, might talk slowly and use few words. A dog, on the other hand, would probably blabber excitedly. He'd also use slang. At least, that's how I imagine these animals would sound. In my poetry, I get to know these people and animals—and I hope you do, too.

If you want to write poetry, here's the best advice I can give. Observe everyone and everything around you. Learn all kinds of things, especially words. The more words you know, the better you can find the best ones to use when you write a poem. Sing and listen to music. Poetry is as much about rhythm as it is about words. Know that there is more than one way to see, hear, say, and imagine anything. Find what is new in every person, animal, place, thing, and, especially, in yourself. Then, sit down and write!

Marilyn Singer

Fog

Trees have no tops
    in the fog
Bridges have no bottoms
Steeples rise like silent rockets
    frozen in space
Street lights float
    like UFOs
No one is your friend
    in the fog
The sky is a liar
The ground is a sneak
All footsteps belong to strangers
    even your own
The fog is
    a river with no direction
    a dream with no doors
When it lifts without a whisper
    you forget that it was ever there
        except for a tiny tickle in your mind
            a trace of goosebumps
                on your skin

MARK VINZ

When I was about the age
you are now,

I didn't care much for poetry. I've come to figure out that it
was because I had a lot of wrong ideas about poetry, from
a lot of different sources. But the main reason was that I
hadn't done enough reading to find out the truth.

I think that's still a problem many people have with
poetry, and that includes some of those who are trying to
write it. They can be bound by their own misconceptions of
what a poem is, and maybe even by some of the stereotypes
that continue to circulate all around us.

A lot of people, for example, think that poetry has to
depend on a kind of fancy language that is found nowhere
else but in poetry—archaic words, flowery words, contrac-
tions such as *ne'er* and *o'er*. Others will tell you that a true
poem is one which is always written in rhyme and meter.
I've met some people, too, who believe that poems must
always be inspirational or always have to do with beauty.
I've heard still others say that a good poem has to be cryptic
or depend heavily on some kind of hidden meaning.

Unfortunately, there are many more examples of this
kind of wrongheadedness, but thankfully, when you start
reading poems, it doesn't take very long to figure out that

poetry is something else entirely. You might begin with some of the great names from the past, such as Walt Whitman, Emily Dickinson, or Robert Frost, and you might continue on to more contemporary writers such as William Stafford or Marge Piercy, or those found in any number of anthologies widely available today. What you'll discover is that while poems always depend on a special use of language, there are many different ways to explore the power of words and sounds, that a poem can be written on just about any subject and with a tremendous variety of forms and approaches.

Finally, I need to come back to reading again, to something that bothers me more than anything else, and that's hearing young writers say that they don't read poems because they don't want to be influenced. I've never heard of musicians who stay away from concerts, or painters refusing to go to art galleries. Why is it that writers can be so afraid of being influenced? Aside from finding out what poems are really all about, and the various ways they can be written, we can read to see how poems open up our own lives to us—to discover what we didn't know we knew, to paraphrase Robert Frost. In short, our reading is the most important place we begin to learn our craft as writers—that long, long road, where it's necessary to have all the help and inspiration we can get!

Mark Vinz

Lilacs

When they came West, the women brought them—
gifts, perhaps, from mothers to daughters
they knew they'd never see again—
for beauty's sake, a piece of home
to plant beside the house or ring a yard,
a shady place to nurture children.

Around the countryside you still
can find them growing wild in clumps
where long ago the farmsteads stood,
reminders of what's lost or hidden—
those final, necessary boundaries
of all that couldn't be cut down.

Sparklers

Twirling our frantic loops and circles,
we cried out *look!* to the grownups
watching from their lawn chairs,
afraid they'd somehow miss the
giddy slash of every turn and leap
until the last glow died and we went back,
warned each time about burnt hands
and bare feet flying in slippery grass.
Again! we shouted, and ran as far
beyond the porch light as we dared,
for this was Independence Day
and we were too busy to listen,
writing our names in thin air.

JANET S. WONG

✂

Try to shout your poems

out on the field, up into a tree. You may look completely stupid, but part of being a poet is being willing to put yourself out there, to open up. Keep the lines of the poem that say what you really need to say, the lines you find yourself shouting extra loud or extra slow. Make them the start of a new draft, a totally different draft. Did you rhyme? For a change, try not to rhyme. Or if you wrote in free verse for the first draft, choose to use rhyme for Draft 2. Maybe try a haiku for Draft 3, or a very long poem for Draft 4, or change voice in Draft 5. I like to knit and splice the best of each draft together. Sometimes the first one is the best, though, so keep them all until you have a stack staring you in the face, and then go back and see where you are.

Some poems seem to beg for the whisper test. The best ones make me smile, or cry, or nod and hum. The best ones make me think, *yes, I know this, too.* They feel like a secret.

I love to write poems because I am lazy. A poem is short. I can write a first draft in five minutes and then go eat a bag of potato chips. Later, when I get another idea, I can

come back and write a second draft in another five minutes.
Five minutes at a time, and the next day I can feel proud of
what I've done. My mind tends to bounce around a lot, and
poems let me follow the crazy bouncing.

Quilt

Our family
is a quilt

of odd remnants
patched together

in a strange
pattern,

threads fraying,
fabric wearing thin—

but made to keep
its warmth

even in bitter
cold.

JANE YOLEN

𝒳

Poets often try to define poetry,

and end up writing poems to do it. It is that hard. In a long poem I wrote among other things that a poem is:

> Emotion surprised.
>
> Throwing a colored shadow.
>
> A word that doubles back on itself, not once but twice.
>
> The exact crunch of carrots.
>
> Precise joys.

The reason we can't define it is that definition and poem both take words. And words are as slippery as fish. Ever watch a bear try to catch a fish? That's a poet, big and clumsy, with strong claws and jaws, after a silver slipcased fish that—once caught—lies lumpen on the shore.

Many of my poems reflect my love of fairy tales and I use those already-well-known characters as a jumping-off place to write about things that have been fretting or gnawing at me. For example, my poem "Gingerbread Boy" was written on a day I felt overwhelmed with responsibilities: I had a long book tour coming up and a revision for a novel not yet finished, my daughter had called saying her daughter was sick and I had no time to fly down to comfort them, and my husband was in the middle of a major problem at the university where he was chairman of the computer science department. I woke up that morning with a refrain running through my head. "Run, run, as fast as you can, You can't catch me, I'm the Gingerbread Man." So many teeth biting at my heels, indeed!

Jane Yolen

Gingerbread Boy

The world is one mouth.
So many teeth bite my heels
I run on my toes.

Stonehenge

The roving people counted moons,
The settled used the sun;
But here eternity's clock is timed
By summer's shadow through the stones.

Who worshipped here within the round?
Who danced the fairy ring?
Whose priestly voices called the tunes?
Whose bodies from the stones were hung?

Earthworks these are, and Earth's remain,
The barrows bound and point
To worlds in worlds we scarcely know
That rain and mist and sun anoint.

Once Upon a Time She Said

"Once upon a time," she said
and the world began anew:
a vee of geese flew by,
plums roasting in their breasts;
a vacant-eyed princess
sat upon a hillock of glass;
a hut strolled through a tangled wood,
the nails on its chickenfeet
blackened and hard as coal;
a horse's head proclaimed advice
from the impost of an arch;
one maiden spoke in toads,
another in pearls,
and a third with the nightingale's voice.
If you ask me,
I would have to say
all the world's magic
comes directly from the mouth.

Notes on Contributors

JOSEPH BRUCHAC is an author, storyteller, and editor who has drawn on his Native American heritage throughout his writing career. He has edited more than thirty books and has written more than sixty books of his own, including *Squanto's Journey; The Boy Who Lived with the Bears*, a *Boston Globe–Horn Book* Honor Book; *Dog People*, winner of the Paterson Children's Writing Award; and *Many Nations: An Alphabet of Native America*, winner of an International Reading Association Teachers' Choice Award. The cofounder of *Greenfield Review Press*, Joseph Bruchac lives with his wife in upstate New York.

SIV CEDERING is an award-winning author, poet, screenwriter, and visual artist. She is also an accomplished composer of music and an illustrator of books for children. Her writing has appeared in numerous anthologies, including *How to Write Poetry*, edited by Paul B. Janeczko, and *What Have You Lost?*, edited by Naomi Shihab Nye. Siv Cedering lives in Amagansett, New York.

KALLI DAKOS worked as an elementary school teacher, a reading specialist, and a freelance writer for newspapers and magazines prior to becoming a poet for children. Her collections *If You're Not Here, Raise Your Hand; Don't Read This Book, Whatever You Do!*; and *The Goof Who Invented Homework* were all praised as IRA Children's Choices Selections. Kalli Dakos divides her time between her homes in Ottawa, Ontario, Canada, and Great Falls, Virginia.

MICHAEL DUGAN worked in bookselling, publishing, and rock music before becoming a full-time writer. He has written numerous books for children, including *No Other Way, Wombats Can't Fly, Unbalanced Poems*, and *The King Who Gobbled His Dinner*. He is also the author of the children's play *Life's a Riot*. Michael Dugan is vice president of the Fellowship of Australian Writers and frequently conducts writing workshops with adults and children. He has also co-edited several anthologies of Australian poetry and spent five years as poetry adviser to the literary quarterly *Overland*. Michael Dugan lives in Melbourne, Australia.

ROBERT FARNSWORTH lives, writes, and teaches in Maine. His poems have appeared widely in magazines throughout the United States, and his two collections, *Three or Four Hills and a Cloud* and *Honest Water*, were published by Wesleyan University Press. Writer-in-Residence at Bates College, Robert Farnsworth also edits poetry for the Washington, D.C., quarterly *The American Scholar*.

RALPH FLETCHER has written numerous books for young readers, including *Ordinary Things: Poems from a Walk in Early Spring; Relatively Speaking: Poems About Family; Spider Boy; Flying Solo;* and *Fig Pudding*, which was named an ALA Notable Children's Book. He has also written many books for writers and writing teachers, such as *What a Writer Needs;* and *Breathing In, Breathing Out: Keeping a Writer's Notebook*. Ralph Fletcher lives with his family in New Hampshire.

DOUGLAS FLORIAN has spent most of his life in New York City, where he was born. He studied art at Queens College and the School of Visual Arts in New York. He is the author and illustrator of many award-winning books for children, including *Mammalabilia; Laugheteria; Beast Feast*, named an ALA Notable Children's Book and winner of a Lee Bennett Hopkins Poetry Award; and *insectlopedia*, named an ALA Notable Children's Book and a Best Book of the Year by both *Publishers Weekly* and *Child* magazine. Douglas Florian lives with his family in New York.

ADAM FORD is co-editor of the Australian literary journals *Going Down Swinging* and *Overland Express* (http://www.overlandexpress.org). His most recent collection of poetry, *Not Quite the Man for the Job*, won the inaugural REACT Top Young Adult Read Award in 1998. He is also the author of the forthcoming novel *Man Bites Dog*. Adam Ford lives in Melbourne, Australia, and works as a freelance editor in between making various magazines and comics for his own amusement (and hopefully the amusement of others).

KRISTINE O'CONNELL GEORGE is the recipient of both the Lee Bennett Hopkins Poetry Award and the International Reading Association's Promising Poet Award for *The Great Frog Race and Other Poems*. Her other titles include *Old Elm Speaks: Tree Poems*, recipient of the SCBWI Golden Kite Award; *Little Dog Poems*, named an ALA Notable Children's Book; *Toasting Marshmallows: Camping Poems; Book!*; and *Little Dog and Duncan*. Kristine O'Connell George teaches poetry writing classes for the UCLA Writers' Program and enjoys meeting fellow poetry lovers through her website, www.kristinegeorge.com.

NIKKI GRIMES is the author of many acclaimed books for children, including *Meet Danitra Brown*, an American Library Association Notable Book and Coretta Scott King Honor Book; *Jazmin's Notebook*, a *Booklist* Editors' Choice, Bank Street College Book of the Year, and Coretta Scott King Honor Book; and *My Man Blue*, a *Booklist* Editors' Choice, Bank Street College Book of the Year, and *Riverbank Review* Children's Book of the Year finalist. Nikki Grimes lives in California.

GEORGIA HEARD has written two children's poetry books, *Creatures of Earth, Sea, and Sky* and *Songs of Myself: An Anthology of Poetry and Art*. She is also the author of *For the Good of the Earth and Sun: Teaching Poetry; Writing Toward Home: Tales and Lessons to Find Your Way*; and *Awakening the Heart: Exploring Poetry in Elementary and Middle School*. Georgia Heard lives with her family in New York.

CHRISTINE HEMP recently launched a poem into space on a NASA mission sent to monitor the prenatal activity of stars. Her poems and commentaries have appeared on National Public Radio, most recently on *Morning Edition*. Her work has appeared in such publications as *Harvard Magazine*, *Yale Angler's Journal*, the *Christian Science Monitor*, and in anthologies by Simon and Schuster and Orchard Press. After years away in New England, Europe, and New Mexico, Christine Hemp moved back to her native Puget Sound in Washington State.

STEVEN HERRICK is one of Australia's most popular and prolific poets for children and young adults. Over the past eleven years, he has written such award-winning books as *Water Bombs*; *My Life, My Love, My Lasagne*; *Love Poems & Leg-Spinners*; and *Poetry to the Rescue*. Three of his verse novels have been short-listed for the Children's Book Council of Australia Book of the Year. Steven Herrick regularly performs his poems throughout Australia in schools, pubs, universities, festivals, and on radio and television. He has also toured Canada, the United Kingdom, the United States, and Singapore. He lives in Australia's Blue Mountains with his partner and two sons.

MARY ANN HOBERMAN is a poet and the critically acclaimed author of many books for children, including *One of Each*, *The Eensy Weensy Spider*, *And to Think That We Thought That We'd Never Be Friends*, and *A House Is a House for Me*, which won a National Book Award. She was also the editor of the poetry anthology *My Song Is Beautiful: Poems and Pictures in Many Voices*. Mary Ann Hoberman gives readings in libraries and schools, and her poems are included in countless anthologies. She lives in Connecticut.

LEE BENNETT HOPKINS has written and edited numerous award-winning books for children and young adults, including *Been to Yesterdays: Poems of a Life*, which received the Christopher Award and was named a Golden Kite Honor Book, and *My America: A Poetry Atlas of the United States*, which was a *Reading Rainbow* featured selection. To encourage the recognition of poetry, he established two major awards: the Lee Bennett Hopkins Poetry Award, presented annually by Penn State University for a single volume of poetry, and the Lee Bennett Hopkins–International Reading Association Promising Poet Award, presented every three years by IRA. Lee Bennett Hopkins divides his time between Westchester County, New York, and Greenwich Village in New York City.

ANDREW HUDGINS is an esteemed poet for adults. His volumes of poetry include *Babylon in a Jar*; *The Glass Hammer: A Southern Childhood*; *The Never-Ending: New Poems*; *After the Lost War: A Narrative*; and *Saints and Strangers*, which was short-listed for the Pulitzer Prize. He is also the author of a book of essays, *The Glass Anvil*. Andrew Hudgins's awards and honors include the Witter Bynner Award for Poetry, the Hanes Poetry Prize, and fellowships from the Bread Loaf Writers' Conference, the Ingram Merrill Foundation, and the National Endowment for the Arts. Andrew Hudgins lives in Ohio.

BOBBI KATZ is the author of numerous books for young readers, including *We the People*, a *Booklist* Editors' Choice; *Upside Down and Inside Out: Poems for All Your Pockets*; *Could We Be Friends? Poems for Pals*; and most recently *A Rumpus of Rhymes: A Book of Noisy Poems*. Her poetry has appeared in many anthologies, such as *The Place My Words Are Looking For*, edited by Paul B. Janeczko. Bobbi Katz lives in New York.

X. J. KENNEDY is an accomplished poet for both adults and children. His books for young readers include *Fresh Brats*, a *Booklist* Editors' Choice and an International Reading Association Children's Choices Award winner; *The Kite That Braved Old Orchard Beach*, a Bank Street College Book of the Year; and *Talking Like the Rain: A Read-to-Me Book of Poems*, an anthology edited with Dorothy M. Kennedy. He is also the recipient of an Award for Excellence in Children's Poetry by the National Council of Teachers of English. X. J. Kennedy lives in Massachusetts.

KARLA KUSKIN is the author and illustrator of more than fifty books for children. Her first book was *Roar and More*. Her other books include *The Philharmonic Gets Dressed*, *The Sky Is Always in the Sky*, and *Soap Soup and Other Verses*. She has received many awards, including the National Council of Teachers of English Award for Excellence in Poetry in 1979. In 1998, she delivered the first annual Charlotte Zolotow Lecture at the University of Wisconsin. Karla Kuskin lives in Brooklyn, New York, and Arlington, Virginia.

J. PATRICK LEWIS is a renowned author of numerous books for children, including *Doodle Dandies*; *Isabella Abnormella and the Very, Very Finicky Queen of Trouble*; *Bloshblobberbosh: Runcible Poems for Edward Lear*; *A Burst of Firsts: Doers, Shakers, Record Breakers*; *Arithmetickle*; *Freedom Like Sunlight: Praisesongs for Black Americans*; *A World of Wonders*; and *The Shoe Tree of Chagrin*. His work has also been included in more than sixty anthologies. J. Patrick Lewis lives in Ohio.

PHOTO: ANN W. OLSON

GEORGE ELLA LYON has published two collections of poems, *Mountain* and *Catalpa*, winner of the Appalachian Book of the Year Award; nineteen picture books, including *Who Came Down That Road?*, a *Publishers Weekly* Best Book of the Year; *Basket*, winner of the Kentucky Bluegrass Award; and *Book*, named a Notable Book by the National Council of Teachers of English. The poem "Where I'm From" was featured on the PBS series *The United States of Poetry*. Her work has also been selected for inclusion in numerous anthologies, such as *Food Fight*, edited by Michael J. Rosen, and *I Feel A Little Jumpy Around You*, edited by Naomi Shihab Nye and Paul B. Janeczko. George Ella Lyon lives in Kentucky.

PHOTO: GLENN WESTON

LILIAN MOORE is the author of many well-known books for children, including *Adam Mouse's Book of Poems*; *Don't Be Afraid, Amanda*; *I Never Did That Before*; *Poems Have Roots*; and *I'm Small*. She is also a recipient of the Award for Excellence in Poetry for Children from the National Council of Teachers of English. Lilian Moore lives in Washington State.

LILLIAN MORRISON has written and edited numerous books for young readers, including *Rhythm Road*, named an American Library Association Best Book for Young Adults and a Notable Children's Book; *Sprints and Distances*, named an American Library Association Notable Children's Book and a *New York Times* Outstanding Book for the Younger Reader; and *I Scream, You Scream*, listed as one of the New York Public Library's 100 Best New Books for Children in 1997. Her poetry has also appeared in many anthologies, most recently *The 20th Century Children's Poetry Treasury*, edited by Jack Prelutsky. Lillian Morrison lives in New York.

NAOMI SHIHAB NYE is the author of many books for children, including *Lullaby Raft*, *Habibi*, and *Sitti's Secrets*, the latter two recipients of the Jane Addams Children's Book Award. She has edited six prize-winning anthologies of poetry for young readers, including *This Same Sky*, *The Tree Is Older Than You Are*, *The Space Between Our Footsteps: Poems and Paintings from the Middle East*, *Salting the Ocean*, and *What Have You Lost?*, which received the Lee Bennett Hopkins Poetry Award. Naomi Shihab Nye lives in Texas.

TOM POW is known as one of the leading poets of Scotland, where he lives and works as a lecturer in Creative and Cultural Studies at Glasgow University, Crichton Campus. He is the recipient of two Scottish Arts Council Book Awards and was short-listed for the Scottish Book of the Year Award. His poetry and prose have appeared in many magazines and journals, including *The New Yorker*. He is the author of two children's books, *Who Is the World For?* and *Callum's Big Day*.

JACK PRELUTSKY was born in Brooklyn, grew up in the Bronx, and ran off to Manhattan. After stints as a cab driver, photographer, folksinger, and more, he is now the award-winning author of more than thirty collections of original verse, including *The New Kid on the Block*, *A Pizza the Size of the Sun*, *It's Raining Pigs and Noodles*, and *Awful Ogre's Awful Day*. In addition, he is the editor of numerous anthologies, including *The Random House Book of Poetry for Children*. Jack Prelutsky and his wife live in Washington State.

LIZ ROSENBERG is an accomplished poet and author, and is the editor of such award-winning anthologies as *Light-Gathering Poems, Earth-Shattering Poems,* and *The Invisible Ladder,* which was a 1997 *Hungry Mind* Book of Distinction. In addition, she is a professor of children's literature and creative writing at SUNY Binghamton. Liz Rosenberg lives with her husband and son in Binghamton, New York.

ALICE SCHERTLE is the author of more than thirty books for children, including *A Lucky Thing; I Am the Cat; How Now, Brown Cow;* and *Advice for a Frog.* She is the recipient of the Christopher Award, an International Reading Association Celebrate Literacy Award, and the Southern California Council on Literature for Children and Young People Award. Many of her books have been honored as American Library Association Notable Books, *School Library Journal* Best Books, and National Council for Teachers of English Notable Books. Alice Schertle lives in Massachusetts.

MARILYN SINGER is the author of more than sixty books for children and young adults. Her works include novels, picture books, nonfiction, and collections of poetry. Many of her poems have been selected for inclusion in such anthologies as *Worst Moments,* edited by Lee Bennett Hopkins; *The 20th Century Children's Poetry Treasury* and *The Beauty of the Beast,* both edited by Jack Prelutsky; *Weird Pet Poems,* edited by Dilys Evans; *Food Fight,* edited by Michael J. Rosen; and *Poetry from A to Z: A Guide for Young Writers,* edited by Paul B. Janeczko. She is also the host of the AOL Children's Writers Chat. Marilyn Singer lives in Brooklyn, New York, and Washington Depot, Connecticut, with her husband and a lot of pets.

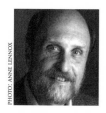

MARK VINZ has taught at Moorhead State University since 1968, where he is currently a professor of English. His poems, stories, and essays for adults have appeared in more than two hundred magazines and anthologies. Mark Vinz's most recent books include *Late Night Calls: Prose Poems and Short Fiction; Minnesota Gothic;* and *Affinities.* He also served as the co-editor of several anthologies of literature, including *Inheriting the Land: Contemporary Voices from the Midwest;*

Imagining Home: Writing from the Midwest; and *The Talking of Hands: Unpublished Writing by New Rivers Press Authors*, all of which won Minnesota Book Awards. Mark Vinz lives in Minnesota.

JANET S. WONG is a graduate of UCLA and Yale Law School, though she gave up her career as a lawyer to write picture books and poetry for children and young adults. She is the author of such books as *Behind the Wheel: Poems About Driving*, named a Quick Pick for Reluctant Readers by the Young Adult Library Services Association; *Buzz*, named one of the Best Books of the Year by *School Library Journal*; and *The Trip Back Home*, winner of the Asian Pacific American Award for Literature. Janet S. Wong lives in Washington State.

JANE YOLEN has written and edited more than two hundred books and anthologies — for all age levels and in genres ranging from picture books to fantasy to science fiction. Her numerous awards include the Christopher Medal for *The Seeing Stick*; the National Jewish Book Award for *The Devil's Arithmetic*; the World Fantasy Award for *Favorite Folktales from Around the World*; and five honors for her body of work in children's literature, including the Kerlan Award, the Keene State College Children's Literature Festival Award, and the Regina Medal. Jane Yolen and her husband divide their time between western Massachusetts and Scotland.

Index of First Lines

Acknowledgments

"Song to the Firefly" copyright © 2002 by Joseph Bruchac. Reprinted by permission of the author.

"Longhouse Song" copyright © 2002 by Joseph Bruchac. Reprinted by permission of the author.

"The Changeling" copyright © 1998 by Siv Cedering. Reprinted by permission of the author.

"Squished Up Pencil" from the forthcoming book *Put Your Eyes Up and Other School Poems* by Kalli Dakos. Copyright © 2002 by Kalli Dakos. Reprinted by permission of Simon & Schuster Books for Young Readers, an imprint of Simon & Schuster Children's Publishing Division.

"My pencil is a mess" and "I may be pretty" copyright © 2002 by Kalli Dakos. Reprinted by permission of the author.

"My Writing Is an Awful Mess" from *Don't Read This Book, Whatever You Do!* by Kalli Dakos. Copyright © 1993 by Kalli Dakos. Reprinted by permission of the author.

"I'd Mark with the Sunshine" from *Don't Read This Book, Whatever You Do!* by Kalli Dakos. Copyright © 1993 by Kalli Dakos. Reprinted by permission of the author.

"Don't Tell Me" copyright © 2002 by Michael Dugan. Reprinted by permission of the author.

"Bleak Prospect" copyright © 2002 by Michael Dugan. Reprinted by permission of the author.

"Yard Sale" copyright © 2000 by Robert Farnsworth. First published in *Sundog: The Southeast Review.* Reprinted by permission of the author.

"Man with a Metal Detector" from *Have You Been to the Beach Lately?* by Ralph Fletcher. Copyright © 2002 by Ralph Fletcher. Published by Orchard Books, an imprint of Scholastic Inc. Reprinted by permission.

"Playing with Fire" from *I Am Wings.* Text copyright © 1994 by Ralph Fletcher. Reprinted with the permission of Atheneum Books for Young Readers, an imprint of Simon & Schuster Children's Publishing Division.

"Bad Poem" from *Laugh-eteria.* Copyright © 1999 by Douglas Florian. Reprinted by permission of Harcourt, Inc.

"The Whirligig Beetles" from *insectlopedia.* Copyright © 1998 by Douglas Florian. Reprinted by permission of Harcourt, Inc.

"Smile" copyright © 2002 by Adam Ford. Reprinted by permission of the author.

"Maple Shoot in the Pumpkin Patch" copyright © 2002 by Kristine O'Connell George. Reprinted by permission of the author.

"The Blue Between" copyright © 2002 by Kristine O'Connell George. Reprinted by permission of the author.

"Sweethearts Dance" copyright © 2002 by Nikki Grimes.

"Dragonfly" copyright © 2002 by Georgia Heard. From *Creatures of Earth, Sea, and Sky,* by Georgia Heard, published by Boyds Mills Press. Reprinted by permission of the author.

"Connecting Cord" copyright © 2002 by Christine Hemp. Reprinted by permission of the author.

"Seeing the World" copyright © by Steven Herrick. From *My Life, My Love, My Lasagne.* Reprinted by permission of University of Queensland Press.

"May Fly" from *The Llama Who Had No Pajama.* Copyright © 1998 by Mary Ann Hoberman. Reprinted by permission of Harcourt, Inc.

"Pick Up Your Room" from *Fathers, Mothers, Sisters, Brothers.* Copyright © 1991 by Mary Ann Hoberman. Reprinted by permission of Little, Brown and Company (Inc.).

"CD a Poem" copyright © 1999 by Lee Bennett Hopkins. First published by the Children's Book Council. Reprinted by permission of Curtis Brown Ltd.

"Subways Are People" copyright © 1971 by Lee Bennett Hopkins. Reprinted by permission of Curtis Brown Ltd.

"Grandmother's Spit" copyright © 1994 by Andrew Hudgins. From *The Glass Hammer* by Andrew Hudgins. Reprinted by permission of Houghton Mifflin Company. Previously published in *The Atlantic.* All rights reserved.